DOVER · THRIFT · EDITIONS

Oscar Wilde's Wit and Wisdom

A Book of Quotations

OSCAR WILDE

DOVER PUBLICATIONS, INC.
Mineola, New York

DOVER THRIFT EDITIONS

GENERAL EDITOR: PAUL NEGRI

Bibliographical Note

Oscar Wilde's Wit and Wisdom is a new selection of quotations, first published by Dover Publications, Inc., in 1998.

Library of Congress Cataloging-in-Publication Data

Wilde, Oscar, 1854–1900.
 [Selections. 1998]
 Oscar Wilde's wit and wisdom : a book of quotations / Oscar Wilde.
 p. cm. — (Dover thrift editions)
 ISBN 0-486-40146-4 (pbk.)
 1. Wilde, Oscar, 1854–1900—Quotations. 2. Quotations, English. I. Title.
II. Series.
PR5812 1998
828'.802—dc21
 98-13741
 CIP

Manufactured in the United States of America
Dover Publications, Inc., 31 East 2nd Street, Mineola, N.Y. 11501

Note

OSCAR WILDE (1854–1900), a leading figure of the art-for-art's-sake movement in late nineteenth-century England, once said "I put all my genius into my life; I put only my talent into my works." Wilde's genius—as well as his talent—was to give memorable and striking expression, through wit and brilliance, to his keen observations on human nature and society in general. For that reason, Wilde's conversation often attained the same high artistic level as his plays, fiction, poetry, criticism and other works. His verbal virtuosity and mental agility, coupled with an ardent disregard for propriety, resulted in a stream of epigrams and aphorisms that were widely quoted in his time and have lost none of their popularity in our own. Wilde is certainly among the most quoted writers in English, perhaps second only to Shakespeare.

Wilde was born in Dublin, the son of prominent parents. He attended Trinity College and later Oxford, where his poetry—as well as his personality—attracted considerable attention, not all of it favorable. Early on he established the role he was to play all his life—the sayer (and doer) of outrageous things, the champion of Art and Beauty, the nemesis of the dull, ordinary, and merely practical, the quintessential aesthete. The success of his novel *The Picture of Dorian Gray* (1891) and his plays *The Importance of Being Earnest* (1895), *Lady Windermere's Fan* (1892), *An Ideal Husband* (1895), among other works, earned him a place among the leading writers of the time. In 1895, at the height of his success, Wilde was charged with and convicted of homosexual practices, bringing a sudden and dramatic end to his brilliant career. After serving two years at hard labor, Wilde was released, but penniless and in broken health, he lived in self-imposed exile and died in Paris in 1900.

Wilde had something witty (and sometimes profound) to say about almost everything. This book includes a wealth of observations on a variety of topics arranged in general categories. The source of the quotation is cited in each case and a list of the works appears on p. 60.

Contents

LIFE

The secret of life is never to have an emotion that is unbecoming. *A Woman of No Importance*.

*

Life is much too important a thing ever to talk seriously about it. *Vera, or The Nihilists*.

*

The Book of Life begins with a man and woman in a garden. It ends with Revelations.
 A Woman of No Importance.

*

One's real life is so often the life that one does not lead. *In Conversation*.

*

To live is the rarest thing in the world. Most people exist, that is all.
 The Soul of Man Under Socialism.

*

To become a spectator of one's own life is to escape the suffering of life.
 The Picture of Dorian Gray.

Life is never fair . . . And perhaps it is a good thing for most of us that it is not.

An Ideal Husband.

*

. . . the world has been made by fools that wise men should live in it.

A Woman of No Importance.

*

There are few things easier than to live badly and to die well. *Vera, or The Nihilists.*

*

One can live for years sometimes without living at all, and then all life comes crowding into one single hour. *Vera, or The Nihilists.*

*

Ambition is the last refuge of the failure.
Phrases and Philosophies for the Use of the Young.

*

Give me the luxuries, and anyone can have the necessaries. *In Conversation.*

*

It is because Humanity has never known where it was going that it has never been able to find its way.
The Critic as Artist.

*

We live in an age that reads too much to be wise, and thinks too much to be beautiful.
The Picture of Dorian Gray.

*

I love acting. It is so much more real than life.
The Picture of Dorian Gray.

One should absorb the colour of life, but one should never remember its details. Details are always vulgar. *The Picture of Dorian Gray.*

*

. . . when the gods wish to punish us they answer our prayers. *An Ideal Husband.*

*

We can have in life but one great experience at best, and the secret of life is to reproduce that experience as often as possible.
 The Picture of Dorian Gray.

*

Ethics, like natural selection, make existence possible. Aesthetics, like sexual selection, make life lovely and wonderful, fill it with new forms, and give it progress, and variety and change.
 The Critic as Artist.

*

Misfortunes one can endure—they come from outside, they are accidents. But to suffer for one's own faults—ah!—there is the sting of life!
 Lady Windermere's Fan.

*

To believe is very dull. To doubt is intensely engrossing. To be on the alert is to live; to be lulled into security is to die. *In Conversation.*

*

In her dealings with man Destiny never closes her accounts. *The Picture of Dorian Gray.*

*

The world is a stage, but the play is badly cast.
 Lord Arthur Savile's Crime.

Good taste is the excuse I've always given for leading such a bad life.

The Importance of Being Earnest.

*

. . . try as we may we cannot get behind things to the reality. And the terrible reason may be that there is no reality in things apart from their appearances.

In Conversation.

*

Life is terribly deficient in form. Its catastrophes happen in the wrong way and to the wrong people. There is a grotesque horror about its comedies, and its tragedies seem to culminate in farce.

The Critic as Artist.

*

I am always astonishing myself. It is the only thing that makes life worth living.

A Woman of No Importance.

*

I wrote when I did not know life; now that I do know the meaning of life, I have no more to write. Life cannot be written; life can only be lived.

In Conversation.

*

The world is simply divided into two classes— those who believe the incredible, like the public— and those who do the improbable.

A Woman of No Importance.

*

The world has always laughed at its own tragedies, that being the only way in which it has been able to bear them.

A Woman of No Importance.

Memory is the diary that we all carry about with us. *The Importance of Being Earnest.*

*

Discontent is the first step in the progress of a man or a nation. *A Woman of No Importance.*

*

We are each our own devil, and we make this world our hell. *The Duchess of Padua.*

*

In Paris one can lose one's time most delightfully; but one can never lose one's way.
In Conversation.

*

But the past is of no importance. The present is of no importance. It is with the future that we have to deal. For the past is what man should not have been. The present is what man ought not to be. The future is what artists are.
The Soul of Man Under Socialism.

*

One can survive everything nowadays, except death, and live down anything except a good reputation. *A Woman of No Importance.*

WOMEN

Women are meant to be loved, not to be understood. *The Sphinx Without a Secret.*

*

Women—Sphinxes without secrets.
A Woman of No Importance.

One should never trust a woman who tells one her real age. A woman who would tell one that, would tell one anything.

A Woman of No Importance.

*

It is perfectly brutal the way most women nowadays behave to men who are not their husbands.

Lady Windermere's Fan.

*

Crying is the refuge of plain women but the ruin of pretty ones. *Lady Windermere's Fan.*

*

Women know life too late. That is the difference between men and women.

A Woman of No Importance.

*

I don't know that women are always rewarded for being charming. I think they are usually punished for it! *An Ideal Husband.*

*

Good women have such limited views of life, their horizon is so small, their interests are so petty.

A Woman of No Importance.

*

She'll never love you unless you are always at her heels; women like to be bothered.

Vera, or The Nihilists.

*

A woman will flirt with anybody in the world as long as other people are looking on.

The Picture of Dorian Gray.

Plain women are always jealous of their husbands. Beautiful women never have time. They are always so occupied in being jealous of other people's husbands. *A Woman of No Importance.*

*

Thirty-five is a very attractive age, London society is full of women of the very highest birth who have, of their own free choice, remained thirty-five for years. *The Importance of Being Earnest.*

*

It takes a thoroughly good woman to do a thoroughly stupid thing. *Lady Windermere's Fan.*

*

Women defend themselves by attacking, just as they attack by sudden and strange surrender.
The Picture of Dorian Gray.

*

Women are a decorative sex. They never have anything to say, but they say it charmingly. Women represent the triumph of matter over mind, just as men represent the triumph of mind over morals.
The Picture of Dorian Gray.

*

Women love us for our defects. If we have enough of them, they will forgive us everything, even our own gigantic intellects.
A Woman of No Importance.

*

I don't believe in women thinking too much. Women should think in moderation, as they should do all things in moderation.
A Woman of No Importance.

Women forgive adoration; that is quite as much as should be expected from them.

A Woman of No Importance.

❋

MRS. ALLONBY: We women adore failures. They lean on us. *A Woman of No Importance.*

❋

She looks like a woman with a past. Most pretty women do. *An Ideal Husband.*

❋

American girls are as clever at concealing their parents as English women are at concealing their past. *The Picture of Dorian Gray.*

❋

Women have no appreciation of good looks; at least good women have not.

The Picture of Dorian Gray.

❋

The one charm of the past is that it is past. But women never know when the curtain has fallen.

The Picture of Dorian Gray.

❋

I am afraid that women appreciate cruelty, down-right cruelty, more than anything else. They have wonderfully primitive instincts. We have emancipated them, but they remain slaves looking for their masters all the same. *The Picture of Dorian Gray.*

❋

Every woman is a rebel, and usually in wild revolt against herself. *A Woman of No Importance.*

Women are not meant to judge us, but to forgive us when we need forgiveness. Pardon not punishment, is their mission. *An Ideal Husband.*

*

Women are the most reliable as they have no memory for the important.
Letter to Robert Ross written from Reading Prison.

*

There is one thing infinitely more pathetic than to have lost the woman one is in love with, and that is to have won her and found out how shallow she is. *In Conversation.*

*

The only way to behave to a woman is to make love to her, if she is pretty, and to some one else, if she is plain. *The Importance of Being Earnest.*

*

MRS. CHEVELEY: The strength of women comes from the fact that psychology cannot explain us. Men can be analysed and women . . . merely adored. *An Ideal Husband.*

*

Being adored is a nuisance. Women treat us just as Humanity treats its Gods. They worship us and are always asking us to do something for them.
The Picture of Dorian Gray.

*

The history of women is the history of the worst form of tyranny the world has ever known. The tyranny of the weak over the strong. It is the only tyranny that lasts. *A Woman of No Importance.*

Women are never disarmed by compliments. Men always are. That is the difference between the sexes. *An Ideal Husband.*

*

The only way a woman can ever reform a man is by boring him so completely that he loses all possible interest in life. *The Picture of Dorian Gray.*

*

It is only very ugly or very beautiful women who ever hide their faces. *The Duchess of Padua.*

*

Women give to men the very gold of their lives. But they invariably want it back in small change.
 In Conversation.

*

Women, as some witty Frenchman once put it, inspire us with the desire to do masterpieces, and always prevent us from carrying them out.
 The Picture of Dorian Gray.

*

She was made to be an ambassador's wife. She certainly has a wonderful faculty of remembering people's names, and forgetting their faces.
 A Woman of No Importance.

*

I am sick of women who love me. Women who hate me are much more interesting.
 The Picture of Dorian Gray.

*

She is a peacock in everything but beauty.
 The Picture of Dorian Gray.

Women have a wonderful instinct about things.
They can discover everything except the obvious.
An Ideal Husband.

*

As long as a woman can look ten years younger
than her own daughter, she is perfectly satisfied.
The Picture of Dorian Gray.

*

Wicked women bother one. Good women bore
one. That is the only difference between them.
Lady Windermere's Fan.

*

There is only one real tragedy in a woman's life.
The fact that her past is always her lover, and her fu-
ture invariably her husband. *An Ideal Husband.*

*

MISS PRISM: A misanthrope I can understand—a
womanthrope, never!
The Importance of Being Earnest.

MEN

Men become old, but they never become good.
Lady Windermere's Fan.

*

No man is rich enough to buy back his past.
An Ideal Husband.

*

The evolution of man is slow. The injustice of
man is great. *The Soul of Man Under Socialism.*

MRS. ALLONBY: I delight in men over seventy, they always offer one the devotion of a lifetime.
 A Woman of No Importance.

*

I sometimes think that God in creating man, somewhat overestimated His ability.
 In Conversation.

*

. . . one is tempted to define man as a rational animal who always loses his temper when he is called upon to act in accordance with the dictates of his reason. *The Critic as Artist.*

*

A man who moralizes is usually a hypocrite, and a woman who moralizes is invariably plain.
 Lady Windermere's Fan.

*

Rich bachelors should be heavily taxed. It is not fair that some men should be happier than others.
 In Conversation.

*

Men are horribly tedious when they are good husbands, and abominably conceited when they are not. *A Woman of No Importance.*

*

When a man acts he is a puppet. When he describes he is a poet. *In Conversation.*

*

What a man really has, is what is in him. What is outside of him should be a matter of no importance.
 The Soul of Man Under Socialism.

MRS. ALLONBY: Man, poor, awkward, reliable, necessary man belongs to a sex that has been rational for millions and millions of years. He can't help himself. It is in his race. The History of Woman is very different. We have always been picturesque protests against the mere existence of common sense. We saw its dangers from the first.
A Woman of No Importance.

*

A bad man is the sort of man who admires innocence, and a bad woman is the sort of woman a man never gets tired of.
A Woman of No Importance.

*

The husbands of very beautiful women belong to the criminal classes. *The Picture of Dorian Gray.*

*

MRS. ALLONBY: The Ideal Man . . . he should always say much more than he means, and always mean much more than he says.
A Woman of No Importance.

*

When a man is old enough to do wrong he should be old enough to do right also.
A Woman of No Importance.

*

He has one of those terribly weak natures that are not susceptible to influence. *An Ideal Husband.*

*

When men give up saying what is charming, they give up thinking what is charming.
Lady Windermere's Fan.

Men who are trying to do something for the world, are always insufferable, when the world has done something for *them*, they are charming.

In Conversation.

*

Man can believe the impossible, but man can never believe the improbable.

The Decay of Lying.

PEOPLE IN GENERAL

People who count their chickens before they are hatched, act very wisely, because chickens run about so absurdly that it is impossible to count them accurately. *Letter from Paris May 1900.*

*

One can always be kind to people about whom one cares nothing. *The Picture of Dorian Gray.*

*

It is absurd to divide people into good and bad. People are either charming or tedious.

Lady Windermere's Fan.

*

I like men who have a future and women who have a past. *The Picture of Dorian Gray.*

*

The more one analyses people, the more all reasons for analysis disappear. Sooner or later one comes to that dreadful universal thing called human nature. *The Decay of Lying.*

Whenever people talk to me about the weather, I always feel certain that they mean something else.
The Importance of Being Earnest.

*

The public have an insatiable curiosity to know everything, except what is worth knowing.
The Soul of Man Under Socialism.

*

Philanthropic people lose all sense of humanity. It is their distinguishing characteristic.
The Picture of Dorian Gray.

*

Most men and women are forced to perform parts for which they have no qualifications.
Lord Arthur Savile's Crime.

*

Nowadays people know the price of everything and the value of nothing.
The Picture of Dorian Gray.

*

Well bred people always stay in exactly the same place as we do. *The Birthday of the Infanta.*

*

I'm sure I don't know half the people who come to my house. Indeed, from all I hear, I shouldn't like to. *An Ideal Husband.*

*

I like persons better than principles and I like persons with no principles better than anything else in the world. *The Picture of Dorian Gray.*

There are only two kinds of people who are really fascinating—people who know absolutely everything and people who know absolutely nothing.

The Picture of Dorian Gray.

*

It is perfectly monstrous the way people go about, nowadays, saying things against one behind one's back that are absolutely and entirely true.

A Woman of No Importance.

*

People who want to say merely what is sensible should say it to themselves before they come down to breakfast in the morning, never after.

In Conversation.

*

Nowadays most people die of a sort of creeping common sense, and discover when it is too late that the only things one never regrets are one's mistakes.

The Picture of Dorian Gray.

LOVE, MARRIAGE

It is difficult not to be unjust to what one loves.

The Critic as Artist.

*

Nothing spoils a romance so much as a sense of humour in the woman—or the want of it in the man. *A Woman of No Importance.*

*

The worst of having a romance of any kind is that it leaves one so unromantic.

The Picture of Dorian Gray.

. . . not love at first sight, but love at the end of the season, which is so much more satisfactory.

Lady Windermere's Fan.

*

Love can canonize people. The saints are those who have been most loved.

Letter to Robert Ross, May 28th 1897.

*

If one really loves a woman, all other women in the world become absolutely meaningless to one.

Lady Windermere's Fan.

*

What a silly thing love is! It is not half as useful as logic, for it does not prove anything and it is always telling one things that are not going to happen, and making one believe things that are not true.

The Nightingale and the Rose.

*

To love oneself is the beginning of a life-long romance.

Phrases and Philosophies for the Use of the Young.

*

. . . love and gluttony justify everything.

In Conversation.

*

Romance is the privilege of the rich, not the profession of the poor. *The Model Millionaire.*

*

Men always want to be a woman's first love. That is their clumsy vanity. Women have a more subtle instinct about things: What they like is to be a man's last romance. *A Woman of No Importance.*

Any place you love is the world to you . . . but love is not fashionable any more, the poets have killed it. They wrote so much about it that nobody believed them, and I am not surprised. True love suffers, and is silent. *The Remarkable Rocket.*

*

One should always be in love. That is the reason one should never marry. *In Conversation.*

*

There is always something ridiculous about the emotions of people whom one has ceased to love.
 The Picture of Dorian Gray.

*

Keep love in your heart. A life without it is like a sunless garden when the flowers are dead. The consciousness of loving and being loved brings a warmth and richness to life that nothing else can bring. *In Conversation.*

*

A man can be happy with any woman as long as he does not love her. *The Picture of Dorian Gray.*

*

When one is in love one begins by deceiving oneself. And ends by deceiving others. That is what the world calls a romance.
 A Woman of No Importance.

*

DUCHESS OF MONMOUTH: . . . We women, as someone says, love with our ears, just as you men love with your eyes, if you ever love at all.
 The Picture of Dorian Gray.

Young men want to be faithful and are not; old men want to be faithless and cannot.
The Picture of Dorian Gray.

*

Always! That is a dreadful word. It makes me shudder when I hear it. Women are so fond of using it. They spoil every romance by trying to make it last for ever. It is a meaningless word too. The only difference between a caprice and a life-long passion is that the caprice lasts a little longer.
The Picture of Dorian Gray.

*

Men marry because they are tired; women because they are curious; both are disappointed.
The Picture of Dorian Gray.

*

The one charm of marriage is that it makes a life of deception absolutely necessary for both parties.
The Picture of Dorian Gray.

*

MRS. ALLONBY: My husband is a sort of promissory note; I'm tired of meeting him.
A Woman of No Importance.

*

For an artist to marry his model is as fatal as for a *gourmet* to marry his cook: the one gets no sittings, and the other no dinner. *In Conversation.*

*

Faithfulness is to the emotional life what consistency is to the life of the intellect—simply a confession of failures. *The Picture of Dorian Gray.*

The very essence of romance is uncertainty. If ever I get married, I'll certainly try to forget the fact.
The Importance of Being Earnest.

*

Once a week is quite enough to propose to anyone, and it should always be done in a manner that attracts some attention. *An Ideal Husband.*

*

It is not the perfect but the imperfect who have need of love. *An Ideal Husband.*

*

. . . in married life three is company and two is none. *The Importance of Being Earnest.*

*

Those who are faithful know only the trivial side of love: it is the faithless who know love's tragedies.
The Picture of Dorian Gray.

*

There is one thing worse than an absolutely loveless marriage. A marriage in which there is love, but on one side only. *An Ideal Husband.*

*

I am not in favour of long engagements. They give people the opportunity of finding out each other's character before marriage, which I think is never advisable. *The Importance of Being Earnest.*

*

The amount of women in London who flirt with their own husbands is perfectly scandalous. It looks so bad. It is simply washing one's clean linen in public. *The Importance of Being Earnest.*

The happiness of a married man depends on the people he has not married.

A Woman of No Importance.

*

If we men married the women we deserve we should have a very bad time of it.

An Ideal Husband.

*

I have always been of the opinion that a man who desires to get married should know either everything or nothing.

The Importance of Being Earnest.

*

The proper basis for marriage is mutual misunderstanding. *Lord Arthur Savile's Crime.*

*

Twenty years of romance make a woman look like a ruin; but twenty years of marriage make her look like a public building.

A Woman of No Importance.

*

In married life affection comes when people thoroughly dislike each other. *An Ideal Husband.*

*

It is the growth of the moral sense in women that makes marriage such a hopeless one-sided institution. *An Ideal Husband.*

*

Englishwomen conceal their feelings till after they are married. They show them then.

A Woman of No Importance.

No man should have a secret from his wife—she invariably finds it out. *In Conversation.*

*

When a woman finds out about her husband she either becomes dreadfully dowdy, or wears very smart bonnets that some other woman's husband has to pay for. *The Picture of Dorian Gray.*

*

There's nothing in the world like the devotion of a married woman. It's a thing no married man knows anything about.

Lady Windermere's Fan.

*

As for domesticity, it ages one rapidly, and distracts one's mind from higher things.

The Remarkable Rocket.

*

When a woman marries again, it is because she detested her first husband. When a man marries again, it is because he adored his first wife. Women try their luck; men risk theirs.

The Picture of Dorian Gray.

*

Her capacity for family affection is extraordinary. When her third husband died, her hair turned quite gold from grief. *The Picture of Dorian Gray.*

*

There is no pleasure in taking in a husband who never sees anything. *The Picture of Dorian Gray.*

PARENTS, RELATIONS, FRIENDSHIP

After a good dinner one can forgive anybody, even one's own relations.

A Woman of No Importance.

*

Extraordinary thing about the lower classes in England—they are always losing their relations. They are extremely fortunate in that respect.

An Ideal Husband.

*

Laughter is not at all a bad beginning for a friendship, and it is far the best ending for one.

The Picture of Dorian Gray.

*

Between men and women there is no friendship possible. There is passion, enmity, worship, love, but no friendship. *Lady Windermere's Fan.*

*

Anybody can sympathize with the sufferings of a friend, but it requires a very fine nature to sympathize with a friend's success.

The Soul of Man Under Socialism.

*

Children begin by loving their parents. After a time they judge them. Rarely, if ever do they forgive them. *A Woman of No Importance.*

All women become like their mothers. That is their tragedy. No man does. That's his.
The Importance of Being Earnest.

*

I think that generosity is the essence of friendship. *The Devoted Friend.*

*

The longer I live the more keenly I feel that whatever was good enough for our fathers is not good enough for us. *The Picture of Dorian Gray.*

*

Relations are simply a tedious pack of people, who haven't got the remotest knowledge of how to live, nor the smallest instinct about when to die.
The Importance of Being Earnest.

*

To lose one parent . . . may be regarded as a misfortune; to lose both looks like carelessness.
The Importance of Being Earnest.

*

One has a right to judge a man by the effect he has over his friends. *The Picture of Dorian Gray.*

*

I always like to know everything about my new friends, and nothing about my old ones.
The Picture of Dorian Gray.

*

I dare say that if I knew him I should not be his friend at all. It is a very dangerous thing to know one's friends. *The Remarkable Rocket.*

She is without one good quality, she lacks the finest spark of decency, and is quite the wickedest woman in London. I haven't a word to say in her favour . . . and she is one of my greatest friends.

In Conversation.

*

I shall never make a new friend in my life, though perhaps a few after I die. *In Conversation.*

YOUTH AND OLD AGE

The old believe everything; the middle-aged suspect everything; the young know everything.
Phrases and Philosophies for the Use of the Young.

*

To get back one's youth, one has merely to repeat one's follies. *The Picture of Dorian Gray.*

*

The tragedy of old age is not that one is old, but that one is young. *The Picture of Dorian Gray.*

*

The soul is born old but grows young. That is the comedy of life. And the body is born young and grows old. That is life's tragedy.

A Woman of No Importance.

*

The youth of the present day are quite monstrous. They have absolutely no respect for dyed hair. *Lady Windermere's Fan.*

Youth is the one thing worth having.
The Picture of Dorian Gray.

*

Youth smiles without any reason. It is one of its chiefest charms. *The Picture of Dorian Gray.*

CONDUCT, MORALS, EXPERIENCE

Nothing looks so like innocence as an indiscretion. *Lord Arthur Savile's Crime.*

*

Moderation is a fatal thing. Nothing succeeds like excess. *A Woman of No Importance.*

*

What people call insincerity is simply a method by which we can multiply our personalities.
The Critic as Artist.

*

. . . my duty is a thing I never do, on principle.
An Ideal Husband.

*

The only thing that ever consoles man for the stupid things he does is the praise he always gives himself for doing them. *In Conversation.*

*

A cynic is a man who knows the price of everything and the value of nothing.
Lady Windermere's Fan.

Any preoccupation with ideas of what is right or wrong in conduct shows an arrested intellectual development.
Phrases and Philosophies for the Use of the Young.

*

To be natural is such a very difficult pose to keep up. *An Ideal Husband.*

*

Let me say to you now that to do nothing at all is the most difficult thing in the world, the most difficult, and the most intellectual.
The Critic as Artist.

*

A sensitive person is one who, because he has corns himself, always treads on other people's toes.
The Remarkable Rocket.

*

. . . duty is what one expects from others, it is not what one does oneself.
A Woman of No Importance.

*

It is always more difficult to destroy than to create, and when what one has to destroy is vulgarity and stupidity, the task of destruction needs not merely courage but also contempt.
The Critic as Artist.

*

He would stab his best friend for the sake of writing an epigram on his tombstone.
Vera, or The Nihilists.

The first duty in life is to be as artificial as possible. What the second duty is no one has yet discovered.
Phrases and Philosophies for the Use of the Young.

*

Dullness is the coming-of-age of seriousness.
Phrases and Philosophies for the Use of the Young.

*

It is always nice to be expected and not to arrive.
An Ideal Husband.

*

One should always be a little improbable.
Phrases and Philosophies for the Use of the Young.

*

We think that we are generous because we credit our neighbours with the possession of those virtues that are likely to be a benefit to us.
In Conversation.

*

Philanthropy seems to me to have become simply the refuge of people who wish to annoy their fellow creatures. *An Ideal Husband.*

*

When we are happy we are always good but when we are good we are not always happy.
In Conversation.

*

To be good is to be in harmony with oneself. Discord is to be forced to be in harmony with others.
In Conversation.

Everyone should keep someone else's diary.
In Conversation.

*

Whenever a man does a thoroughly stupid thing,
it is always from the noblest of motives.
The Picture of Dorian Gray.

*

A little sincerity is a dangerous thing, and a great
deal of it is absolutely fatal. *The Critic as Artist.*

*

There is a fatality about good resolutions—they
are always made too late.
The Picture of Dorian Gray.

*

One should always play fairly—when one has the
winning cards. *An Ideal Husband.*

*

Being natural is simply a pose, and the most irri-
tating pose I know. *The Picture of Dorian Gray.*

*

I don't like principles . . . I prefer prejudices.
An Ideal Husband.

*

I never put off till tomorrow what I can possibly
do—the day after. *In Conversation.*

*

I rely on you to misrepresent me.
In Conversation.

I am but too conscious of the fact that we are born in an age when only the dull are treated seriously, and I live in terror of not being misunderstood. *The Critic as Artist.*

*

Moderation is a fatal thing. Enough is as bad as a meal. More than enough is as good as a feast.
 The Picture of Dorian Gray.

*

. . . all influence is bad, but a good influence is the worst in the world.
 A Woman of No Importance.

*

A good reputation is one of the many annoyances to which I have never been subjected.
 A Woman of No Importance.

*

There *is* a good deal to be said for blushing, if one can do it at the proper moment.
 A Woman of No Importance.

*

One should never make one's *debut* with a scandal. One should reserve that to give an interest to one's old age. *The Picture of Dorian Gray.*

*

All ways end at the same point . . . Disillusion.
 The Picture of Dorian Gray.

*

Morality is simply the attitude we adopt to people whom we personally dislike. *An Ideal Husband.*

It is personalities, not principles, that move the age. *In Conversation.*

*

I never came across anyone in whom the moral sense was dominant who was not heartless, cruel, vindictive, log-stupid, and entirely lacking in the smallest sense of humanity. Moral people, as they are termed, are simple beasts. I would sooner have fifty unnatural vices than one unnatural virtue.
 In Conversation.

*

It is not good for one's morals to see bad acting.
 The Picture of Dorian Gray.

*

Experience is the name every one gives to their mistakes. *Lady Windermere's Fan.*

*

Personal experience is a most vicious and limited circle. *The Decay of Lying.*

SIN, RELIGION, TRUTH

He hasn't a single redeeming vice.
 In Conversation.

*

You will soon be going about like the converted, and the revivalist, warning people against all the sins of which you have grown tired.
 The Picture of Dorian Gray.

Nothing makes one so vain as being told that one is a sinner. *The Picture of Dorian Gray.*

*

Starvation, and not sin, is the parent of modern crime. *The Soul of Man Under Socialism.*

*

Sin is a thing that writes itself across a man's face. It cannot be concealed.
The Picture of Dorian Gray.

*

I can resist everything except temptation.
Lady Windermere's Fan.

*

Wickedness is a myth invented by good people to account for the curious attractiveness of others.
Phrases and Philosophies for the Use of the Young.

*

. . . there are terrible temptations that it requires strength, strength and courage to yield to.
An Ideal Husband.

*

If your sins find you out, why worry! It is when they find you *in*, that trouble begins.
In Conversation.

*

Life's aim, if it has one, is simply to be always looking for temptations. There are not nearly enough. I sometimes pass a whole day without coming across a single one. It is quite dreadful. It makes one so nervous about the future.
A Woman of No Importance.

Every impulse that we strive to strangle broods in the mind and poisons us . . . The only way to get rid of temptation is to yield to it. *In Conversation.*

*

The only difference between the saint and sinner is that every saint has a past, and every sinner has a future. *A Woman of No Importance.*

*

There is no sin except stupidity.
 The Critic as Artist.

*

One should believe evil of everyone, until, of course, people are found out to be good. But that requires a great deal of investigation nowadays.
 A Woman of No Importance.

*

Scepticism is the beginning of Faith.
 The Picture of Dorian Gray.

*

Religions die when they are proved to be true. Science is the record of dead religions.
Phrases and Philosophies for the Use of the Young.

*

If one tells the truth, one is sure, sooner or later, to be found out.
Phrases and Philosophies for the Use of the Young.

*

The truth is rarely pure and never simple. Modern life would be very tedious if it were either, and modern literature a complete impossibility.
 The Importance of Being Earnest.

It is the confession, not the priest that gives us absolution. *The Picture of Dorian Gray.*

*

Religion is the fashionable substitute for Belief.
 The Picture of Dorian Gray.

*

Prayer must never be answered: if it is, it ceases to be prayer and becomes correspondence.
 In Conversation.

*

Most religious teachers spend their time trying to prove the unproven by the unprovable.
 In Conversation.

*

It is a terrible thing for a man to find out suddenly that all his life he has been speaking nothing but the truth. *The Importance of Being Earnest.*

GENIUS, THOUGHT, BEAUTY

Geniuses . . . are always talking about themselves, when I want them to be thinking about me.
 An Ideal Husband.

*

The public is wonderfully tolerant. It forgives everything except genius. *The Critic as Artist.*

*

I like looking at geniuses, and listening to beautiful people. *An Ideal Husband.*

Would you like to know the great drama of my life? It is that I have put my genius into my life—I have put only my talent into my works.

In Conversation.

*

Genius is born, not paid. *In Conversation.*

*

I know so many men in London whose only talent is for washing. I suppose that is why men of genius so seldom wash; they are afraid of being mistaken for men of talent only! *In Conversation.*

*

The worst thing you can do for a person of genius is to help him: that way lies his destruction. I have had many devoted helpers—and you see the result.

In Conversation.

*

I think that it is better to be beautiful than to be good. But on the other hand no one is more ready than I am to acknowledge that it is better to be good than to be ugly. *The Picture of Dorian Gray.*

*

Good looks are a snare that every sensible man would like to be caught in.

The Importance of Being Earnest.

*

All beautiful things belong to the same age.

Pen, Pencil and Poison.

*

She has the remains of really remarkable ugliness.

In Conversation.

All thought is immoral. Its very essence is destruction. If you think of anything, you kill it. Nothing survives being thought of.

A Woman of No Importance.

*

The value of an idea has nothing whatsoever to do with the sincerity of the man who expresses it.

The Picture of Dorian Gray.

*

Yes: I am a dreamer. For a dreamer is one who can only find his way by moonlight, and his punishment is that he sees the dawn before the rest of the world. *The Critic as Artist*.

*

Consistency is the last refuge of the unimaginative.

In Conversation.

ART, LITERATURE, MUSIC, CRITICISM

It is only an auctioneer who can equally and impartially admire all schools of Art.

The Critic as Artist.

*

All art is immoral. For emotion for the sake of emotion is the aim of art, and emotion for the sake of action is the aim of life. *The Critic as Artist*.

*

We live in an age when men treat art as if it were meant to be a form of autobiography.

The Picture of Dorian Gray.

We can forgive a man for making a useful thing as long as he does not admire it. The only excuse for making a useless thing is that one admires it intensely.
All art is quite useless.
The Picture of Dorian Gray.

*

The true artist is a man who believes absolutely in himself, because he is absolutely himself.
The Soul of Man Under Socialism.

*

Most of our modern portrait painters are doomed to oblivion. They never paint what they see. They paint what the public sees, and the public never sees anything. *The Decay of Lying.*

*

The Academy is too large and too vulgar. Whenever I have gone there, there have been either so many people that I have not been able to see the pictures, which was dreadful or so many pictures that I have not been able to see the people, which was worse.
The Picture of Dorian Gray.

*

Paradox though it may seem—and paradoxes are always dangerous things—it is none the less true that life imitates art far more than art imitates life.
The Decay of Lying.

*

The proper school to learn art is not Life but Art.
The Decay of Lying.

*

Art is our spirited protest, our gallant attempt to teach Nature her proper place.
The Decay of Lying.

Bad artists always admire each other's work. They call it being large-minded and free from prejudice. But a truly great artist cannot conceive of life being shown, or beauty fashioned, under any conditions other than those he has selected.

The Critic as Artist.

*

To reveal art and conceal the artist is art's aim.

The Picture of Dorian Gray.

*

No great artist ever sees things as they really are. If he did he would cease to be an artist.

The Decay of Lying.

*

There are two ways of disliking art . . . One is to dislike it. The other is to like it rationally.

The Critic as Artist.

*

Whistler left America in order to remain an artist, and Mr. Sargent to become one. *In Conversation.*

*

It is the spectator, and not life, that art really mirrors.

The Picture of Dorian Gray.

*

The Artist is the creator of beautiful things.

The Picture of Dorian Gray.

*

I never travel without my diary. One should always have something sensational to read in the train.

The Importance of Being Earnest.

The only portraits in which one believes are portraits where there is very little of the sitter and a very great deal of the artist. *The Decay of Lying.*

*

Popularity is the crown of laurel which the world puts on bad art. Whatever is popular is wrong.
 Lecture to Art Students.

*

That poetic school of artists who imagine that the true way of idealising a sitter is to paint someone else. *In Conversation.*

*

Only mediocrities progress. An artist revolves in a cycle of masterpieces, the first of which is no less perfect than the last. *In a Newspaper Article.*

*

That curious mixture of bad painting and good intentions that always entitles a man to be called a representative British artist. *In Conversation.*

*

To fail and to die young is the only hope for a Scotsman who wishes to remain an artist.
 In Conversation.

*

M. ZOLA is determined to show that, if he has not got genius, he can at least be dull.
 The Decay of Lying.

*

Only the great masters of style ever succeed in being obscure.
Phrases and Philosophies for the Use of the Young.

Whistler is indeed one of the very greatest masters of painting in my opinion. And I may add that in this opinion Mr. Whistler himself entirely concurs.

From the Pall Mall Gazette.

*

There is no such thing as a moral or an immoral book. Books are well written or badly written. That is all. *The Picture of Dorian Gray.*

*

On George Moore:
He leads his readers to the latrine and locks them in. *In Conversation.*

*

MR. HENRY JAMES, writes fiction as if it were a painful duty.

The Decay of Lying.

*

Between them Hugo and Shakespeare have exhausted every subject. Originality is no longer possible—even in sin. So there are no real emotions left—only extraordinary adjectives.

In Conversation.

*

The books that the world calls immoral books are books that show the world its own shame.

The Picture of Dorian Gray.

*

I hate vulgar realism in literature. The man who could call a spade a spade should be compelled to use one. It is the only thing he is fit for.

The Picture of Dorian Gray.

MR. JAMES PAYN is an adept in the art of concealing what is not worth finding. *The Decay of Lying.*

*

I write because it gives me the greatest possible artistic pleasure to write. If my work pleases the few I am gratified. As for the mob, I have no desire to be a popular novelist. It is far too easy.

Reply to a Critic.

*

—can be read without any trouble and was probably written without any trouble also!

As a Reviewer.

*

. . . a form of poetry which cannot possibly hurt anybody, even if translated into French.

Review in Pall Mall Gazette.

*

We have been able to have fine poetry in England because the public do not read it, and consequently do not influence it.

The Soul of Man Under Socialism.

*

There are two ways of disliking poetry, one way is to dislike it, the other is to read Pope.

In Conversation.

*

They lead us through a barren desert of verbiage to a mirage that they call life . . . However, one should not be too severe on English novels; they are the only relaxation of the intellectually unemployed.

Review in Pall Mall Gazette.

On Charles Dickens:
One must have a heart of stone to read the death of Little Nell without laughing. *In Conversation.*

*

Anybody can write a three-volumed novel. It merely requires a complete ignorance of both life and literature. *The Critic as Artist.*

*

If one cannot enjoy reading a book over and over again, there is no use in reading it at all.
 The Decay of Lying.

*

The aim of most of our modern novelists seems to be, not to write good novels, but to write novels that will do good. *As a Reviewer.*

*

Poets know how useful passion is for publication. Nowadays a broken heart will run to many editions.
 The Picture of Dorian Gray.

*

A poet can survive anything but a misprint.
 In Conversation.

*

Literature always anticipates life. It does not copy it, but moulds it to its purpose. The nineteenth century, as we know it, is largely an invention of Balzac.
 The Decay of Lying.

*

. . . if one plays good music people don't listen, and if one plays bad music people don't talk.
 The Importance of Being Earnest.

After playing Chopin, I feel as if I had been weeping over sins that I had never committed, and mourning over tragedies that were not my own. Music always seems to me to produce that effect. It creates for one a past of which one has been ignorant and fills one with a sense of sorrows that have been hidden from one's tears. *The Critic as Artist.*

*

Musical people are so absurdly unreasonable. They always want one to be perfectly dumb at the very moment when one is longing to be absolutely deaf. *An Ideal Husband.*

*

I like Wagner's music better than anybody's. It is so loud that one can talk the whole time without people hearing what one says.

The Picture of Dorian Gray.

*

. . . the first duty of an art critic is to hold his tongue at all times, and upon all subjects.

The English Renaissance of Art.

*

I am always amused by the silly vanity of those writers and artists of our day who seem to imagine that the primary function of the critic is to chatter about their second-rate work. *The Critic as Artist.*

*

It is exactly because a man cannot do a thing that he is the proper judge of it. *The Critic as Artist.*

*

Criticism demands infinitely more cultivation than creation does. *The Critic as Artist.*

I never reply to my critics. I have far too much time. But I think some day I will give a general answer in the form of a lecture, which I shall call "Straight Talks to Old Men." *In an Interview.*

CONVERSATION, ADVICE, EDUCATION

There is only one thing in the world worse than being talked about, and that is not being talked about. *The Picture of Dorian Gray.*

*

I may have said the same thing before . . . But my explanation, I am sure, will always be different.
 In Conversation.

*

Murder is always a mistake . . . One should never do anything that one cannot talk about after dinner.
 The Picture of Dorian Gray.

*

I love scandals about other people, but scandals about myself don't interest me. They have not got the charm of novelty. *The Picture of Dorian Gray.*

*

A man who allows himself to be convinced by an argument is a thoroughly unreasonable person.
 An Ideal Husband.

*

I dislike arguments of any kind. They are always vulgar, and often convincing.
 The Importance of Being Earnest.

I don't at all like knowing what people say of me behind my back. It makes one far too conceited.

An Ideal Husband.

*

Everything you have said to-day seems to me excessively immoral. It has been most interesting, listening to you. *A Woman of No Importance.*

*

Gossip is charming! . . . History is merely gossip. But scandal is gossip made tedious by morality.

Lady Windermere's Fan.

*

I like to do all the talking myself. It saves time and prevents arguments. *The Remarkable Rocket.*

*

Lots of people act well but very few people talk well, which shows that talking is much more the difficult thing of the two, and much the finer thing also. *The Devoted Friend.*

*

I like talking to a brick wall, it's the only thing in the world that never contradicts me.

Lady Windermere's Fan.

*

Conversation should touch everything but should concentrate itself on nothing.

The Critic as Artist.

*

I hate people who talk about themselves, as you do, when one wants to talk about oneself, as I do.

The Remarkable Rocket.

Questions are never indiscreet. Answers sometimes are. *An Ideal Husband.*

*

The value of the telephone is the value of what two people have to say. *In Conversation.*

*

It is much more difficult to talk about a thing than to do it. In the sphere of actual life that is of course obvious. Anybody can make history. Only a great man can write it. *The Critic as Artist.*

*

She doesn't care much for eloquence in others. She thinks it a little loud. *An Ideal Husband.*

*

Oh, I'm so glad you've come. There are a hundred things I want not to say to you.
 In Conversation.

*

The well-bred contradict other people. The wise contradict themselves.
Phrases and Philosophies for the Use of the Young.

*

It is perfectly monstrous the way people go about nowadays saying things against one behind one's back that are absolutely and entirely true.
 The Picture of Dorian Gray.

*

I always pass on good advice. It is the only thing to do with it. It is never any use to oneself.
 An Ideal Husband.

Don't be conceited about your bad qualities. You
may lose them as you grow old.

A Woman of No Importance.

*

Never try to pull down public monuments such
as the Albert Memorial and the Church. You are
sure to be damaged by the falling masonry.

In Conversation.

*

Never buy a thing you don't want merely because
it is dear. *In Conversation.*

*

Wilde's advice, to a youth who had been told that
he must begin at the bottom, was—"No, begin at
the top and sit upon it." *In Conversation.*

*

Don't be led astray into the paths of virtue.

In Conversation.

*

One should never take sides in anything. Taking
sides is the beginning of sincerity and earnestness
follows shortly afterwards, and the human being be-
comes a bore. *A Woman of No Importance.*

*

Education is an admirable thing, but it is well to
remember from time to time that nothing that is
worth knowing can be taught. *The Critic as Artist.*

*

When people agree with me I always feel that I
must be wrong. *The Critic as Artist.*

About advice:
People are very fond of giving away what they need most themselves. It is what I call the depths of generosity. *The Picture of Dorian Gray.*

*

The mind of a thoroughly well-informed man is a dreadful thing. It is like a bric-à-brac shop, all monsters and dust, with everything priced above its proper value. *The Picture of Dorian Gray.*

*

Give children beauty, not the record of bloody slaughters and barbarous brawls, as they call history, or of the latitude and longitude of places nobody cares to visit, as they call geography.
 A Lecture in America.

*

To have been well brought up is a great drawback nowadays. It shuts one out from so much.
 A Woman of No Importance.

*

To know everything about oneself one must know all about others. *The Critic as Artist.*

WEALTH, POVERTY, SOCIETY

Young people, nowadays, imagine that money is everything, and when they grow older they know it.
 The Picture of Dorian Gray.

*

There is always more brass than brains in an aristocracy. *Vera, or The Nihilists.*

I don't want money. It is only people who pay
their bills who want that, and I never pay mine.
The Picture of Dorian Gray.

*

It is better to have a permanent income than to
be fascinating. *The Model Millionaire.*

*

There is only one class in the community that
thinks more about money than the rich, and that is
the poor. The poor can think of nothing else.
The Soul of Man Under Socialism.

*

I should fancy that the real tragedy of the poor is
that they can afford nothing but self-denial.
The Picture of Dorian Gray.

*

Sometimes the poor are praised for being thrifty.
But to recommend thrift to the poor is both grotesque
and insulting. It is like advising a man who is starving
to eat less. *The Soul of Man Under Socialism.*

*

As for begging it is safer to beg than to take, but it
is finer to take than to beg.
The Soul of Man Under Socialism.

*

I am never in during the afternoon, except when
I am confined to the house by a sharp attack of
penury. *Letter from Paris, May 1898.*

*

Never speak disrespectfully of society. Only peo-
ple who can't get into it do that. *In Conversation.*

If one could only teach the English how to talk, and the Irish how to listen, society here would be quite civilised. *An Ideal Husband*.

*

Society often forgives the criminal; it never forgives the dreamer. *The Critic as Artist*.

JOURNALISM, POLITICS, HISTORY

Patriotism is the virtue of the vicious.
In Conversation.

*

The newspapers chronicle with degrading avidity the sins of the second-rate, and with the conscientiousness of the illiterate give us accurate and prosaic details of the doings of people of absolutely no interest whatever. *In Conversation*.

*

Wherever there is a man who exercises authority, there is a man who resists authority!
The Soul of Man Under Socialism.

*

High hopes were once formed of democracy; but democracy means simply the bludgeoning of the people by the people for the people.
The Soul of Man Under Socialism.

*

Only people who look dull ever get into the House of Commons, and only people who are dull ever succeed there. *An Ideal Husband*.

As one reads history . . . one is absolutely sickened, not by the crimes that the wicked have committed, but by the punishments that the good have inflicted; and a community is infinitely more brutalized by the habitual employment of punishment than it is by the occasional occurrence of crime.

In Conversation.

*

With regard to modern journalists, they always apologize to one in private for what they have written against one in public.

The Soul of Man Under Socialism.

*

Journalism is unreadable, and literature is not read. *The Critic as Artist.*

*

All authority is quite degrading. It degrades those who exercise it, and it degrades those over whom it is exercised. *The Soul of Man Under Socialism.*

*

Modern journalism, by giving us the opinions of the uneducated, keeps us in touch with the ignorance of the community. *The Critic as Artist.*

*

As long as war is regarded as wicked, it will always have its fascination. When it is looked upon as vulgar it will cease to be popular. *The Critic as Artist.*

*

Journalism justifies its own existence by the great Darwinian principle of the survival of the vulgarest.

In Conversation.

The one duty we owe to history is to rewrite it.
 The Critic as Artist.

ENGLAND and AMERICA

England will never be civilized until she has
added Utopia to her dominions.
 The Critic as Artist.

*

I don't desire to change anything in England ex-
cept the weather. *The Picture of Dorian Gray.*

*

The English have a miraculous power of turning
wine into water. *In Conversation.*

*

One of those characteristic British faces that,
once seen are never remembered.
 In Conversation.

*

On arrival in America:
I am not exactly pleased with the Atlantic, it is
not so majestic as I expected. *In Conversation.*

*

On the return voyage:
The Atlantic has been greatly misunderstood.
 In Conversation.

*

We have really everything in common with
America nowadays, except, of course, language.
 The Canterville Ghost.

Somehow I don't think I shall live to see the new century—if another century began and I was still alive, it would really be more than the English could stand. *In Conversation.*

*

In America life is one long expectoration.
 In Conversation.

*

Many American ladies on leaving their native land adopt an appearance of chronic ill-health, under the impression that it is a form of European refinement. *The Canterville Ghost.*

*

Washington has too many bronze generals.
 In Conversation (America).

*

I would rather have discovered Mrs. Langtry than have discovered America. *In Conversation.*

VARIOUS TOPICS

It is only the shallow people who do not judge by appearances. *The Picture of Dorian Gray.*

*

One should either be a work of art, or wear a work of art.
Phrases and Philosophies for the Use of the Young.

*

An egg is always an adventure: it may be different.
 In Conversation.

He has nothing, but looks everything. What more can one desire?

The Importance of Being Earnest.

*

She wore far too much rouge last night and not quite enough clothes. That is always a sign of despair in a woman. *An Ideal Husband.*

*

Fashion is what one wears oneself. What is unfashionable is what other people wear.

An Ideal Husband.

*

In matters of grave importance, style, not sincerity, is the vital thing.

The Importance of Being Earnest.

*

I have made an important discovery . . . that alcohol, taken in sufficient quantities, produces all the effects of intoxication. *In Conversation.*

*

When I am in really great trouble, as anyone who knows me intimately will tell you, I refuse everything except food and drink.

The Importance of Being Earnest.

*

It is very poor consolation to be told that the man who has given one a bad dinner, or poor wine, is irreproachable in private life. Even the cardinal virtues cannot atone for half-cold entrées.

The Picture of Dorian Gray.

"Oh, he occasionally takes an alcoholiday."
A *remark concerning his brother's fondness for drink.*

*

There are many things that we would throw away,
if we were not afraid that others might pick them
up. *The Picture of Dorian Gray.*

*

Selfishness is not living as one wishes to live, it is
asking others to live as one wishes to live.
 The Soul of Man Under Socialism.

*

Illness of any kind is hardly a thing to be encour-
aged in others. Health is the primary duty of life.
 Lady Windermere's Fan.

*

An inordinate passion for pleasure is the secret of
remaining young. *Lord Arthur Savile's Crime.*

*

I adore simple pleasures, they are the last refuge
of the complex. *A Woman of No Importance.*

*

It is better to take pleasure in a rose than to put its
root under a microscope. *In Conversation.*

*

Work is the curse of the drinking classes.
 In Conversation.

*

It is always with the best intentions that the worst
work is done. *The Critic as Artist.*

A mask tells us more than a face.
 Pen, Pencil and Poison.

*

The most comfortable chair is the one I use myself when I have visitors. *An Ideal Husband.*

*

One knows so well the popular idea of health. The English country-gentleman galloping after a fox— the unspeakable in full pursuit of the uneatable.
 A Woman of No Importance.

*

It is mentally and morally injurious to a man to do anything in which he does not find pleasure, and many forms of labour are quite pleasureless activities and should be regarded as such . . . Man is made for something better than disturbing dirt. All work of that kind should be done by a machine.
 The Soul of Man Under Socialism.

*

I was working on the proof of one of my poems all the morning, and took out a comma. In the afternoon I put it back again. *In Conversation.*

*

Industry is the root of all ugliness.
Phrases and Philosophies for the Use of the Young.

*

Cultivated leisure is the aim of man.
 The Soul of Man Under Socialism.

*

One could never pay too high a price for any sensation. *The Picture of Dorian Gray.*

There is something tragic about the enormous number of young men there are in England at the present moment who start life with perfect profiles, and end by adopting some useful profession.
Phrases and Philosophies for the Use of the Young.

*

If there was less sympathy in the world there would be less trouble in the world.
 An Ideal Husband.

*

There is always something infinitely mean about other people's tragedies.
 The Picture of Dorian Gray.

*

I consider ugliness a kind of malady, and illness and suffering always inspire me with revulsion. A man with the toothache ought, I know, to have my sympathy, for it is a terrible pain, yet he fills me with nothing but aversion. He is tedious; he is a bore; I cannot stand him; I cannot look at him; I must get away from him. *In Conversation.*

*

I am afraid I play no outdoor games at all, except dominoes . . . I have sometimes played dominoes outside French cafés. *In Conversation.*

*

I am always thinking about myself, and I expect everybody else to do the same. That is what is called sympathy. *The Remarkable Rocket.*

*

Moods don't last. It is their chief charm.
 A Woman of No Importance.

It is only shallow people who require years to get rid of an emotion. A man who is master of himself, can end a sorrow as easily as he can invent a pleasure.
The Picture of Dorian Gray.

*

A woman's life revolves in curves of emotion. It is upon lines of intellect that a man's life progresses.
An Ideal Husband.

*

. . . a sentimentalist is simply one who desires to have the luxury of an emotion without paying for it.
In Conversation.

*

When one pays a visit it is for the purpose of wasting other people's time, not one's own.
An Ideal Husband.

*

Punctuality is the thief of time—I am not punctual myself, but I do like punctuality in others.
In Conversation.

Bibliography

Quotations in this volume are taken from the following
works of Oscar Wilde

The Duchess of Padua. Methuen, London, 1907.

The Happy Prince and Other Tales (The Happy Prince;
The Nightingale and the Rose; The Selfish Giant;
The Devoted Friend; The Remarkable Rocket). David
Nutt, 1888.

An Ideal Husband; a play. Leonard Smithers, 1899.

The Importance of Being Earnest; A Trivial Comedy for
Serious People. Leonard Smithers, 1899.

Intentions (The Decay of Lying; Pen, Pencil and Poison;
The Critic as Artist; The Truth About Masks). James
R. Osgood McIlvaine, 1891.

Lady Windermere's Fan; a Play about a Good Woman.
Elkin Matthews and John Lane, 1893.

Lord Arthur Savile's Crime and Other Stories (Lord
Arthur Savile's Crime; The Sphinx Without a Secret;
The Canterville Ghost; The Model Millionaire).
James R. Osgood McIlvaine, 1891.

Phrases and Philosophies for the Use of the Young. *The
Chameleon*, December, 1894.

The Picture of Dorian Gray. Ward Lock, 1891.

Salomé (translated from the French by Lord Alfred Douglas). Elkin Matthews and John Lane, 1894.

The Soul of Man Under Socialism. *The Fortnightly Review*, February, 1891.

Vera, or The Nihilists. Ranken & Co., London, 1880.

A Woman of No Importance; a play. John Lane, 1894.